THE LIPSTICK EFFECT

WHY SMALL LUXURIES MEAN BIG PROFITS DURING A RECESSION

DONOVAN GARETT

AlgoRhythms Studios, Ltd.

P.O. BOX 35643

Cleveland, Ohio 44135

United States of America

PRINT ISBN: 978-1-963267-24-2

E-BOOK ISBN: 978-1-963267-25-9

AUDIOBOOK ISBN: 978-1-963267-26-6

Library of Congress Control Number: 2024924308

Printed in the United States of America

Contents

Chapter One

What is the Lipstick Effect?

I FIRST LEARNED ABOUT the *"lipstick effect"* many years ago while doing research for another book. I was instantly fascinated by this business phenomenon and immediately wondered how I could share this with more small business owners who don't really grasp the significance or sales implications of this powerful concept.

So, after toying with the idea for several years, I decided to finally write this book.

When the overall economy takes a plunge, consumer behavior defies conventional expectations. Rather than halting all discretionary spending, people tend to indulge in small luxuries—purchases that bring comfort, enjoyment, and a sense of normalcy without breaking the bank. This behavior, known as the *"lipstick effect,"* has been observed for nearly a century and is a powerful example of how psychology drives spending decisions in financially challenging times.

In this chapter, we'll look at why consumers reach for affordable luxuries during recessions and other stressful economic times, diving into the psychology behind their desire for small comforts. We'll also trace the history of the lipstick effect from the Great Depression down to modern times. By understanding the factors that fuel this effect, you'll better understand the underlying motivations behind your customers' shopping choices.

Throughout this book, you'll see how the *"lipstick effect"* can be a roadmap for creating products and experiences that resonate with buyers on a deep emotional level, no matter what the economy brings.

I'm thrilled and humbled to be a part of your journey.

Let's begin.

Understanding the Lipstick Effect

The *"lipstick effect"* describes the tendency to continue or increase the purchases of small, affordable luxuries in times of financial stress. When the economy declines, consumers often cut back on major expenditures. However, they still want small comforts that bring joy, normalcy, or a boost in confidence. This behavior reflects a deep-seated desire to maintain a sense of control and pleasure in daily life.

The term "*lipstick effect*" was popularized by Leonard Lauder, chairman of Estée Lauder, who observed that lipstick sales increased during times of economic hardship. Lauder's theory was that in uncertain times, people still crave items that offer comfort and self-expression, but in ways that are financially viable. This simple yet telling observation highlighted a core truth about consumer psychology, showing that affordable luxuries have a unique staying power, even when larger purchases may be postponed or foregone altogether.[1]

While lipstick is often used as the prime example, the effect applies to a broad range of affordable luxuries. Beauty products, like lipsticks and skincare items, tend to symbolize the effect because they are accessible, personal, and have an immediate impact on how consumers feel about themselves. They allow people to experience an uplifting sense of control over their appearance, creating a feeling of empowerment that can be especially comforting in challenging economic times.

However, the principle also extends to other small indulgences like premium coffee, scented candles, or imported, high-quality chocolate—any item that serves as a minor "splurge." The lipstick effect demonstrates that, while consumers may adjust their spending, the human desire for comfort, pleasure, and self-care remains constant.

The Psychology Behind the Lipstick Effect

The lipstick effect is rooted in consumer psychology, specifically how people respond to stress, uncertainty, and financial strain. When people face economic hardship, they shift their spending patterns to include smaller, more affordable indulgences. These purchases create a psychological buffer against the stress of larger financial insecurities.

This tendency is tied closely to a phenomenon psychologists refer to as *compensatory consumption*. When faced with limitations in one area, such as budget restrictions, individuals may seek out rewards in other forms to restore a sense of balance or satisfaction.

Small treats—like a new lipstick, a specialty coffee, or a luxury chocolate bar—act as rewards that offer immediate emotional gratification. They provide a feeling of achievement and allow consumers to momentarily escape larger financial worries.[2] These small purchases symbolize normalcy, allowing them to reclaim a sense of control over their lives.

Emotional satisfaction is also central to the appeal of affordable luxuries. When consumers buy something that feels like a treat, it creates a temporary mood boost, enhancing their self-esteem and sense of well-being. These items become sources of *"affordable escapism,"* offering positive feelings without feeling guilt from overspending.

This effect is especially strong in recessions when people feel like they're sacrificing in other areas. A minor indulgence, especially one connected to self-expression or self-care, can feel more like an act of self-preservation, a way of nurturing oneself within the constraints of a tighter budget.

Behavioral economics also sheds light on why the lipstick effect remains a common response to financial stress. When money is tight, people often turn to cognitive shortcuts to justify spending on small luxuries. This *"treat-yourself"* mentality is supported by what economists refer to as *mental accounting*.[3]

People tend to categorize expenses into separate *"mental accounts,"* justifying small, pleasurable purchases as being mentally separate from larger, more necessary expenses. By compartmentalizing minor indulgences, consumers can enjoy them without feeling guilt or shame. This justifies their purchase of small luxuries and also allows them to feel a sense of reward while tightening their spending in other areas.

Together, consumer psychology, emotional satisfaction, and behavioral economic theories explain the lipstick effect. In uncertain times, small indulgences offer a feeling of control, satisfaction, and self-worth—powerful tools for coping with economic stress.

Why the Lipstick Effect Matters: Economic and Business Significance

The lipstick effect is more than just a quirk of consumer psychology; it's a powerful indicator of economic sentiment. It tells us a story about consumer confidence. It reveals that while consumers may be cautious, they're not entirely retreating from the market. Instead, they're adjusting their spending habits, choosing products that deliver comfort, joy, or a sense of self-expression at a manageable price.

Economists view this as a signal that consumer resilience persists, even during economic downturns. When small luxuries continue to see constant demand, it indicates that consumers still have confidence in their ability to handle everyday expenses, just with a different approach.[4]

For business owners (especially small business owners), understanding the lipstick effect can provide a strategic advantage. By recognizing these behaviors, they can adjust their products and services to meet customers where they are.

This adaptable approach allows them to keep existing customers who may be tightening their budgets and attract new customers seeking quality but less expensive treats. Small shifts in product lines, marketing messaging, or even packaging can reposition a brand as an affordable source of comfort, supporting customer loyalty and growing the customer base.[5]

The lipstick effect affects some industries more than others, specifically those associated with self-care, minor indulgences, or personal expression. Cosmetics are the classic example—lipsticks, fragrances, and skincare products see steady demand during recessions, as these items allow consumers to feel good about themselves without a major financial commitment. However, the effect is also visible in other areas, such as entertainment, dining, and personal care.

Streaming services, for instance, commonly experience growth during downturns as people look for affordable ways to unwind at home. Likewise, in dining, specialty coffees and desserts remain popular as they offer moments of pleasure and comfort. These sectors tend to show resilience even when other industries struggle, as they satisfy a fundamental need for affordable luxury, providing a way to maintain normalcy despite broader financial concerns.

The Lipstick Effect Through History

The lipstick effect is not a recent phenomenon. Its roots trace back to some of the most challenging economic times in modern history, where it has consistently indicated how consumers adapt their spending habits when times get tough.

During tough economic times, consumers have invariably turned to affordable luxuries to maintain a sense of normalcy, comfort, and even optimism, demonstrating the reliability of this trend.

The Great Depression and World War II

During the Great Depression of the 1930s, although many industries experienced severe declines, low-cost luxury items and entertainment saw steady or even increased demand. Despite widespread financial hardship, people continued to indulge in small comforts like lipstick, affordable home decor, and going to the cinema. For many, these purchases offered brief moments of relief from the bleak realities of the time.[6]

Similarly, during World War II, when resources were strictly rationed, the demand for small indulgences prevailed. In the United States and Britain, beauty products like lipstick were marketed as morale boosters, and in the face of financial and social constraints, women continued to buy these items as symbols of resilience and self-expression.[7]

The 2008 Financial Crisis

The 2008 financial crisis brought the lipstick effect back into focus, as consumers worldwide adjusted their spending to cope with the economic downturn. Many people avoided large purchases in favor of more affordable indulgences. Beauty products, particularly lipsticks and skincare items, saw a surprising rise in sales, as these items offered a small yet meaningful escape from intense financial stress.[8]

Comfort foods, like artisanal pasta and specialty chocolates, also gained popularity, providing consumers with an accessible luxury to enjoy despite strained budgets. Activities like streaming services and affordable dining options also became preferred choices, allowing people to indulge and relax while on a budget.

The COVID-19 Pandemic

The COVID-19 pandemic presented another, perhaps even stronger, example of the lipstick effect in action. As millions faced lockdowns, job uncertainties, and economic instability, consumer spending patterns shifted noticeably toward small comforts. Beauty products, while limited in physical retail spaces, saw a boom in online sales as people sought ways to feel good at home.[9] Additionally, items that offered physical comfort, like loungewear, scented candles, and premium snacks, surged in popularity as people transformed their living spaces into safe, comforting environments.

Streaming services and at-home entertainment options also thrived, as people found affordable ways to pass the time and stay entertained during times of isolation.

Once again, these small indulgences served as emotional lifelines, providing a sense of control and comfort amid unprecedented global uncertainty.

The lipstick effect has thus proven to be a remarkably consistent consumer behavior across nearly a century of economic hardship. In each historical recession, small luxuries have offered a sense of continuity and control, allowing people to find solace in affordable indulgences. For businesses, these examples illustrate the enduring value of offering products that fulfill this need, demonstrating resilient strategies that weather economic turmoil.

Different Forms of Affordable Luxury

While lipstick stands as the iconic symbol of this phenomenon, the lipstick effect applies broadly to any product or service that offers a touch of affordable indulgence. This pattern means that a wide array of products—not just cosmetics—fall under the category of affordable luxury.

From gourmet coffee to small decor items, inexpensive skincare, and even books, the lipstick effect encompasses a wide range of products that help people experience small moments of satisfaction during economic uncertainty.

Not Just Lipstick

Affordable luxuries take many forms, catering to the diverse needs and preferences of consumers wanting a temporary minor escape from life. For instance, comfort foods like premium chocolate, gourmet snacks, specialty teas, colognes, and similar products have long been popular as they provide a sensory experience that feels indulgent yet is budget-friendly.

Similarly, small home decor items, such as candles, throw pillows, or houseplants, become increasingly popular during economic downturns as people focus on creating comforting environments without overspending. These items, though varied, all share a common trait: they are easy to purchase on a limited budget yet provide a feeling of luxury, comfort, and self-care.

From "Big Wins" to "Small Wins"

During times of economic stress, people often psychologically adjust from aiming for major milestones to seeking small victories or comforts. Behavioral psychologists refer to this shift as the *"small wins"* approach, where minor, easily achievable pleasures become sources of satisfaction and emotional reward.[10] In a stable economy, consumers may look toward saving for large purchases, like vacations, luxury items, or high-end dining experiences.

However, in downturns, these larger purchases are often put on hold, replaced by items that satisfy the desire for a "win" on a smaller scale. A cup of coffee from a favorite café, a book by a beloved author, or a soothing scented candle all deliver a similar boost to morale, but in a way that fits a tighter budget. These small wins serve as achievable, comforting goals that help individuals maintain a sense of normalcy and personal satisfaction, reinforcing the lipstick effect across product categories.

Understanding the many forms that affordable luxury can take helps businesses of all sizes to adapt their product lines and marketing strategies to meet consumers' needs for small comforts. In doing so, they appeal to their customers' desire for minor, attainable pleasures that promote emotional well-being, even though times may be financially challenging.

As we'll see in the following chapters, aligning products with the lipstick effect offers a powerful approach to supporting both customer needs and long-term business goals.

Debunking Myths About the Lipstick Effect

The lipstick effect, while widely recognized, is often misunderstood. There are several misconceptions about what it means and how it works, particularly when applied to various demographics and consumer behaviors. Dispelling these myths helps us gain a clearer picture of why the lipstick effect endures and how it impacts shoppers.

Myth #1: People Only Buy Essentials in Recessions

One common misconception is that during recessions, people abandon all non-essential spending and focus exclusively on necessities. In reality, while consumers do tend to reduce large or luxury-based purchases, many still seek small indulgences that improve their day-to-day experience, often without even consciously realizing it. Affordable moments of joy allow people to retain a sense of normalcy and control, which acts as an emotional stabilizer, bringing comfort in the midst of economic stress.

Psychological studies show that people turn to affordable indulgences as a form of "*mood maintenance,*" helping them cope with financial pressures without committing to a major purchase.[11] They understand that cutting back on big-ticket items is financially prudent, but affordable treats that lift their spirits remain within reach and provide a needed boost to their well-being. This reflects a careful balance of practicality and the innate human desire for pleasure and comfort.

Myth #2: The Lipstick Effect Is Only About Women

Another widespread myth is that the lipstick effect is exclusively tied to women's spending, specifically in beauty and cosmetics. While the term originated in the context of lipstick sales, men also exhibit this behavior in their own spending habits. For men, small indulgences might include a favorite snack, a monthly subscription of craft beers, a magazine subscription, or even low-cost items related to a personal hobby, like fishing gear, grilling accessories, or car care products.[12]

The need for affordable luxury is gender-neutral, driven by a desire to maintain morale during difficult times. Men, like women, are drawn to products that provide minor pleasures and offer a break from financial worri es.[13]

Myth #3: The Lipstick Effect is Obsolete

Some assume that the lipstick effect is an outdated concept. However, the effect is very much alive in modern consumer behavior, as recent trends clearly demonstrate. During the COVID-19 pandemic, for example, sales of affordable self-care and wellness products surged as people looked for ways to feel good and stay comfortable at home. Items such as face masks, aromatherapy oils, and even at-home exercise equipment became popular purchases. Similarly, low-cost streaming services saw record subscriptions as people turned to entertainment as a form of affordable escapism.

These examples illustrate that while the specific products may evolve over time, the core behavior remains. Today, the lipstick effect encompasses a wide array of goods and services, from wellness and self-care to digital entertainment. The modern iteration of the lipstick effect may look different than it did decades ago. Still, it continues to reflect the same fundamental principle: finding comfort from affordable pleasures when times are tough.

By debunking these myths, we gain a clearer understanding of the lipstick effect as a powerful, adaptable response to economic hardship. Recognizing that this behavior extends beyond basic needs, transcends gender, and remains applicable today, entrepreneurs can better align their business and marketing strategies with the ongoing human desire for small comforts.

How the Lipstick Effect Empowers Businesses

For small business owners, understanding the lipstick effect is empowering. Acknowledging that consumers crave affordable luxuries during economic downturns opens opportunities for innovation, strategic positioning, and stronger customer connections. Businesses that harness this knowledge can create products and experiences that resonate deeply with their audience, even when larger purchases are off the table.

Innovate in Changing Markets

Small businesses are uniquely positioned to innovate quickly and effectively in response to shifting consumer behaviors. By applying the principles of the lipstick effect, entrepreneurs can better align their products or services with their desire for affordable comfort.

These adjustments generally don't require a complete overhaul; instead, they need to echo a thoughtful understanding of what customers are seeking—small pleasures that brighten their day without significant cost. This allows businesses to pivot their strategy in a way that directly caters to customers' needs. In turn, their marketing feels personal and timely, helping them stand out in a crowded market.

Building a Brand with Emotional Appeal

Affordable luxuries succeed because they offer more than just another product—they provide an emotional experience. This emotional resonance is especially important during economic downturns when customers want products that bring comfort, self-care, or small moments of joy.

Businesses that understand this can build brands that evoke these emotions, creating a strong bond with consumers who appreciate that the brand just *"gets it."* For instance, a skincare brand that stresses self-care as an everyday ritual or a bakery that promotes its treats as a *"small bite of happiness"* is positioning itself as more than a transactional business; it becomes relationship-focused and a source of comfort.

As a small business owner, building a brand that connects emotionally with your customers is a direct pathway to loyalty and resilience. When customers feel understood, they're more likely to return to brands that support their needs in both good and challenging times. By crafting messaging and products that speak to the universal desire for small indulgences, you can establish your business as a reliable source of affordable comfort.

Understanding the lipstick effect, therefore, provides a roadmap to thrive, even during economic uncertainty. By focusing on affordable luxuries and building a brand with emotional appeal, your business can connect with customers on a meaningful level, turning short-term challenges into long-term opportunities.

In the next chapter, we'll take a look at why the lipstick effect is a powerful predictor of sales trends and economic indicators.

Chapter Two

How the Lipstick Effect Predicts Sales

THE LIPSTICK EFFECT OFFERS more than just a brief glimpse into consumer behavior—it serves as a reliable barometer for broader economic trends. When consumers gravitate toward affordable luxuries in times of financial uncertainty, they reveal what matters most to them: comfort, self-expression, and small moments of joy that fit within a limited budget. These spending habits, while seemingly minor, can tell us a great deal about the larger economic landscape and evolving consumer priorities.

In this chapter, we'll explore why the lipstick effect is such a powerful predictor of sales. As we explore how this phenomenon reflects shifts in consumer confidence, you'll see how it can help your business anticipate demand. By understanding these trends, the lipstick effect can be leveraged strategically, transforming consumer behaviors into actions that drive resilience and growth.

The Power of Predicting Consumer Behavior

In a tough economy, predicting consumer behavior becomes essential. Knowing what your customers want, and are likely to buy, keeps your product line relevant and appealing. Anticipating market shifts also allows your brand to align products with what matters most to your customers, making it easier to maintain customer loyalty and drive steady sales.

The lipstick effect is one of the most dependable signals of changing consumer priorities. As economic pressures rise, behaviors shift toward affordable indulgences that bring comfort without a hefty price tag.

How the Lipstick Effect Reflects Consumer Confidence

The lipstick effect gives us unique insights into consumer confidence, especially during times of financial uncertainty. When the overall economy tightens, a willingness to spend on minor indulgences indicates a level of caution rather than a complete halt in spending. In this way, small purchases act as markers of consumer sentiment, revealing that while people may feel the strain, they are not entirely withdrawing from the economy.

These affordable luxuries also provide a sense of psychological safety. When consumers purchase small indulgences—whether it's a new lipstick, a favorite snack, or a special coffee—they feel as though they're reclaiming a bit of control in an otherwise uncertain world.

Tracking these patterns over time shows a type of consumer confidence that's both cautious and resilient. When spending on small luxuries remains steady or even grows, it reflects a willingness to invest in happiness and normalcy. For businesses, this consistent demand for affordable pleasures is a valuable sign: consumers are still engaged, and there's an opportunity to connect with them meaningfully by offering products that satisfy these needs.

Economic Indicators and the Lipstick Effect

While traditional economic indicators, such as unemployment rates, consumer spending reports, and inflation metrics, provide a broad view of economic health, they often miss finer details of consumer spending, like the specific adjustments consumers make in response to financial stress. The lipstick effect offers a unique lens through which to understand these subtleties. By closely examining these minor purchases, the lipstick effect provides insights into how consumers personally deal with economic downturns.

Economists and analysts pay close attention to the lipstick effect because it can signal shifts in consumer sentiment that broader indicators may overlook. When sales of affordable luxuries stay steady or increase during tough times, it suggests that while consumers are cautious, they still feel comfortable enough to splurge on minor indulgences.

This reflects a form of cautious optimism—a sign that consumers are adjusting but not completely pulling back from spending. In contrast, a corresponding decrease in small luxury spending may suggest deeper financial anxiety, potentially foreshadowing more severe economic impacts.

Industries Most Affected by the Lipstick Effect

The lipstick effect has the most recognizable influence on industries that offer consumers a way to indulge affordably. Not surprisingly, the beauty industry is the most classic example of the lipstick effect in action. Consumers gravitate toward small items such as lipsticks, skincare products, and affordable fragrances, as they provide a quick boost in mood and confidence at a relatively low cost.

The food and beverage sector, specifically items like premium chocolates, gourmet coffee, premium ice cream, and other small treats, also reflects the lipstick effect. When economic stress rises, people often turn to comfort foods to brighten their day.[14] These items provide a measure of escapism and pleasure without financial strain.

Likewise, people look for inexpensive entertainment and comfort. Streaming services, books (especially romance novels), inexpensive home decor items, and cozy household products all see strong sales as part of the lipstick effect. [15] These products satisfy the need for enjoyment and relaxation at a reasonable cost, making them examples of the lipstick effect in action.

Finally, low-cost alternatives to high-end goods provide budget-conscious consumers a luxury experience at a fraction of the price, revealing shifts in spending priorities. [16] From designer-inspired handbags to high-quality skincare clones, these 'dupes' allow consumers to enjoy a taste of luxury on a budget. This trend has grown recently as consumers look for creative ways to meet their desire for quality and style without committing to high-end price tags, as consumers pivot towards savvy, affordable brands.

Trends That Accompany the Lipstick Effect

Alongside the industries impacted by the lipstick effect, several complementary consumer trends also emerge, revealing how people seek comfort and value during economic uncertainty. These trends also highlight a shift in priorities as consumers look for products that are affordable and aligned with their personal values.

Experience-Based Spending

One complementary trend is a preference for minor indulgences that offer lasting experiences rather than single-use luxuries. Instead of buying a one-time luxury item, consumers increasingly turn to experience-based spending that provides ongoing enjoyment.[17] A popular example is signing up for a premium coffee subscription, monthly gift boxes, or an affordable streaming service.

These choices allow consumers to enjoy continuous, high-quality experiences in a financially manageable way. In turn, consumers not only benefit from multiple uses but also enjoy the added value of anticipation and routine enjoyment, which can also provide emotional comfort during stressful times.

Sustainability and Conscious Spending

Increasingly, consumers are more conscious about their spending choices, seeking brands that align with sustainable or ethical practices. During economic downturns, shoppers often engage in *"conscious consumerism,"* gravitating toward brands that make them feel personally fulfilled and socially responsible.[18]

This reflects a desire for “feel-good” purchases—products that not only deliver a sense of indulgence but also align with a buyer’s values, making the purchase feel rewarding on multiple levels. As people look for ways to support causes they care about without overspending, conscious spending and sustainable options become more attractive.

These trends highlight the evolving priorities that generally accompany the lipstick effect. By recognizing these complementary behaviors, you can better connect with your customers, offering products that fulfill both their desire for affordable indulgence and the need for ethical, responsible choices.

Predicting Broader Economic Trends

The lipstick effect does more than just capture immediate consumer behavior; it can also give some insight into broader economic trends. By analyzing shifts in small luxury spending, both business owners and economic analysts can gauge how consumers are responding to changing financial conditions, allowing for a nuanced view of the economy's trajectory.

Lagging Indicator vs. Leading Indicator

In a very real sense, the lipstick effect can function as both a lagging and a leading economic indicator, depending on the stage of an economic downturn. In the early phases of economic decline, the lipstick effect often acts as a lagging indicator. Consumers initially maintain their usual spending habits on larger items until the financial strain becomes more apparent, and then they gradually shift towards smaller, affordable luxuries to cope with the downturn.

As the economy begins to stabilize or show early signs of recovery, the lipstick effect can serve as a leading indicator. When consumers continue to spend on small luxuries or gradually increase their discretionary purchases, it signals renewed confidence and suggests that they feel optimistic enough to make minor indulgences again. This shift often foreshadows broader economic improvement, meaning that consumers are starting to feel secure enough to reintroduce non-essential spending.

Shifts in Spending Priorities

The types of small luxuries consumers gravitate toward during downturns can also signal deeper economic trends. For instance, if consumers begin opting for even lower-cost items or focus solely on essentials, it suggests that financial conditions are worsening, and discretionary spending is at a minimum.

Conversely, steady or increasing sales of affordable luxuries may indicate resilience in consumer sentiment. Watching these shifts provides valuable insight into the intensity of economic strain: resilient spending on minor indulgences indicates cautious optimism, while a strong shift towards essentials reflects more profound financial insecurity.

Predicting Sales in Your Business

As we will discuss in detail in the next chapter, the lipstick effect can be a practical tool for anticipating your consumers' needs and staying relevant during changing economic conditions. This allows you to better position your business to capture demand for small luxuries before your competitors.

The first step is to identify which of your products could be considered *"affordable luxuries"*—items that customers might reach for as a small indulgence during difficult times. Look for products that provide comfort, pleasure, or a sense of self-care while being affordable.

For instance, if you run a coffee shop, premium coffee blends or a unique dessert may fit this category. In retail, items like cozy home decor, quality skincare, or specialty food items often meet the criteria. Think carefully about what makes your customers feel treated, and focus on highlighting those products to align with the lipstick effect.

Once you've identified your affordable luxuries, consider how you can adjust your marketing to capture the essence of the lipstick effect. Position these products as small comforts that bring value, even when budgets are tight. Use language that emphasizes self-care, everyday indulgence, or small rewards that help customers feel good.

For instance, marketing messages like *"A little luxury for your daily routine"* or *"Treat yourself to comfort without breaking the bank"* resonate with shoppers who are mindful of their spending but still want affordable pleasures. By aligning your messaging to highlight the emotional value of these products, you connect with customers on a deeper level and reinforce their appeal.

Recognizing When to Shift Focus

The lipstick effect can ebb and flow, and it's important to recognize when consumer priorities may be shifting. Pay attention to sales trends and monitor customer preferences. If you notice a drop in demand for small luxuries or a rise in sales of more practical, budget-friendly items, it may signal that consumers are focusing more on essentials.

When this happens, consider shifting your focus to products like versatile or multipurpose items. The goal is to pivot your marketing and sales strategy to reflect the current economic climate, making sure products remain timely, relevant, and appealing to customers. By staying responsive and flexible, you not only strengthen customer loyalty but also position your brand as one that adapts thoughtfully to meet people where they are.

In the next chapter, we'll move from theory to practice, diving into specific strategies for applying the lipstick effect in your business. You'll learn how to use insights from this chapter to develop, market, and sell products that align with consumers' desire for small indulgences, ensuring your business remains both relevant and appealing.

Chapter Three

Applying the Lipstick Effect in Your Business

Understanding the lipstick effect is one thing; putting its principles into action is another. Knowing how to adapt your product lines, messaging, and customer experience is a powerful way to build market resilience during a recession.

In this chapter, we'll discuss how to leverage the lipstick effect in your business. Aligning products with your customers' preferences positions your brand as a trusted source of value and satisfaction, even in tough economic times.

Identify Your "Lipstick" Products

Leveraging the lipstick effect begins by recognizing which of your existing products (or services) represent small indulgences that customers find valuable and affordable. This may also mean sourcing new products that align with the principles of the lipstick effect.

Start by assessing your current product lineup to identify items that could be positioned as affordable luxuries. Look carefully for items that:

- Are low-cost compared to other products in your line but are (or, generally perceived to be) high-quality.
- Provide comfort, pleasure, or a feeling of self-care.
- Deliver a unique experience that makes customers feel special or comforted.

These are usually products that may not be essential but offer practical or emotional value at a price point that feels attainable.

If you don't already have products that naturally align with the lipstick effect, consider introducing low-cost options that provide the same sense of affordable indulgence. For instance, a skincare brand could offer travel-sized versions of its bestsellers, giving customers a chance to enjoy a quality product without the full-sized price.

If you're in a service-based industry, consider introducing a budget-friendly option. For example, a spa might offer a quick relaxation treatment or a shorter facial experience, allowing clients to enjoy a luxury experience at a lower price point. This keeps customers engaged with your brand and reinforces its message as a source of value, enjoyment, and emotional support.

Upsells, Cross-Sells, and Growth Strategies

Identifying your business's "lipstick" products is only the beginning; strategic upselling, cross-selling, and bundling can also drive growth. By pairing these sales strategies with your product line, you can increase the value of each customer interaction and build stronger brand loyalty.

The Upsell: Offer Premium or Enhanced Products

Upselling involves offering a slightly more premium version or added feature of a product your customer is already interested in, enhancing their experience without overwhelming their budget.

Restaurants and Cafes: If a customer orders a basic latte, you could offer an upsell to a "deluxe" version with added flavors, specialty milk, or a unique garnish for a modest bump in price.

Personal Care and Beauty: When a customer buys a basic or travel-size skincare product, upsell them to a duo or a "mini kit" that includes a complementary product, giving them more perceived value.

Retail and Home Decor: For small decor items, such as candles, consider an upsell to a larger, longer-lasting version or a set that provides added ambiance.

Upselling works well with "lipstick" products because customers already see the value in these items and are generally agreeable to minor upgrades that enhance their overall experience. By keeping these upsells reasonably priced, you can increase average transaction value without discouraging budget-conscious customers.

The Cross-Sell: Complementary Products

Cross-selling focuses on recommending products that pair well with the customer's original purchase, encouraging them to buy related items that complement their selection. This enhances customer satisfaction, as the recommendations enrich their experience with your products.

Restaurants and Cafes: If a customer orders a coffee, you might suggest a pastry or dessert that complements it, creating a small *"indulgence bundle."*

Personal Care and Beauty: A skincare purchase can be cross-sold with complementary items, such as a facial brush or a travel pouch, enhancing the use of the product.

Retail and Fashion: If a customer buys a small home decor item, you could recommend a complementary item, like a coordinating candle or a decorative throw pillow that enhances the overall ambiance.

Cross-selling is particularly effective because customers are already in a buying mindset. By suggesting a related item that pairs well with their initial choice, you can boost sales while enhancing customer satisfaction.

Limited-Time Offers and Loyalty Rewards

In addition to upsells and cross-sells, consider limited-time offers and loyalty rewards that encourage repeat purchases. Offering discounts on your "lipstick" products or rewards for repeat purchases helps to build long-term relationships while keeping customers 'hooked' on your brand.

Combining sales strategies helps you maximize revenue while providing a product line that resonates with the desire for affordable luxury. These tactics allow you to turn small purchases into touchpoints that strengthen customer loyalty and drive growth.

Create Marketing Messages that Resonate

Successful marketing in a tough economy means speaking directly to your customers' needs for comfort, value, and reassurance. Focusing on themes of self-care, quality, and empathy will help you create messaging that draws attention to your products and strengthens the emotional connection with your audience.

Appeal to Comfort and Self-Care

In times of financial strain, customers want small ways to bring a little comfort into their lives. Your marketing should emphasize how your products are sources of comfort and self-care, focusing on the emotional value they bring.

Highlight small joys: Use phrases like *"Bring a touch of comfort to your day"* or *"Find a moment of calm and happiness."*

Emphasize self-care: Position your products as small yet impactful ways to prioritize wellness and joy. For example, a skincare brand might say, *"A small ritual for a brighter day,"* reminding customers that their purchase is an act of self-nurturing.

Focus on mental and emotional appeal: Messaging like *"A little luxury for your everyday routine"* or *"Treat yourself to a comforting escape"* can create an emotional link between the product and the feeling of warmth or relaxation it provides.

This type of messaging directly aligns with the lipstick effect by framing products as affordable indulgences that add meaning and value to customers' lives despite difficult times.

Focus on Value Without Sacrificing Quality

Even when budgets are tight, consumers are cognizant of value; they just don't want to sacrifice quality or lifestyle. Be sure to craft your messaging to communicate that your products are well-made, high-quality, and provide a worthwhile experience, all at an affordable price.

Position products as affordable investments: Phrases like *"Quality you can feel, at a price you'll love,"* suggest that customers are making a savvy choice without compromising.

Showcase durability and satisfaction: Words like *"lasting quality"* or *"crafted for comfort"* can reinforce that even smaller purchases can bring satisfaction and hold value over time.

Frame products as affordable indulgences: Try positioning your products as *"Affordable luxuries worth every penny"* or *"Everyday comforts without having to splurge."* This communicates that the customer can experience something special without stretching their budget.

Using Empathetic and Relatable Language

Empathy is essential when communicating with customers who may be dealing with financial worries. Your marketing should reflect an understanding of their situation. Keep the tone supportive, encouraging, and relatable.

Acknowledge their reality: Use phrases like *"We know times are tough"* or *"In moments like these, the little things matter."* This approach shows customers that you understand their challenges, promoting a sense of trust.

Present your products as affordable treats: Messages such as *"A small treat to brighten your day"* or *"Treat yourself, without the guilt"* help frame your products as a low-cost way to lift their spirits.

Include an optimistic tone: Language that inspires hope, like *"Brighten every day with a little self-care"* or *"Enjoy a bit of happiness, anytime,"* can remind customers of the power of small comforts to improve their day.

By using empathetic language, you acknowledge your customers' financial concerns while promoting your products as affordable ways to enjoy life's small pleasures. This makes your messaging feel thoughtful and relevant, creating a connection that naturally encourages loyalty.

Marketing messages that speak to comfort, value, and empathy allow you to resonate with customers on a deeper emotional level, aligning your products with their need for affordable, meaningful indulgences. This strengthens the customer relationship and helps position your brand as a source of happiness when it's needed most.

Price Items for Budget-Conscious Consumers

Not surprisingly, the right pricing strategy can make your products more appealing to budget-conscious customers without reducing their perceived value. Thoughtfully pricing items and offering flexible payment options will also help attract consumers.

Create a "sweet spot" for pricing: Items priced between $10 and $30, for instance, often feel more like "small indulgences" and less like significant expenses. Research suggests that *"charm pricing"*—keeping items just under round numbers—encourages spending while still conveying quality. [19]

Offer tiered pricing options: Add different sizes or versions of popular products, allowing customers to experience products at different price levels.

Flexible Payment Models

For higher-cost items or services, consider offering flexible payment solutions that help consumers access your products without a significant upfront financial commitment.

Installment payments: Allowing customers to split payments over several months can make certain items more accessible. Payment platforms like Affirm, Afterpay, Klarna, and PayPal Credit are popular options for breaking up costs.

Subscription models: For consumable or replenishable items, adding a subscription option can offer a slight discount, regular delivery, and convenience. This model not only adds value but also builds a long-term relationship with customers, as they continually receive their favorite products at regular intervals.

"Try before you buy" options: For products where customers may hesitate to invest upfront, offering a trial period or sample program can give them confidence in their purchase. If they enjoy the product, they're more likely to continue and even upgrade.

Flexible payment options provide a more attractive value proposition for budget-conscious shoppers. This allows them to experience your products without financial strain, enhancing their satisfaction and loyalty to your brand.

Product Packaging and Presentation

The way your product is packaged and presented is also an important part of the customer experience. Packaging and presentation can enhance the perceived value of even the most budget-friendly items, making them feel special and more indulgent.

Budget-friendly packaging doesn't have to look cheap. Consumers often look for affordable luxuries that still feel high-quality, so consider packaging that is simple yet visually appealing.

Choose minimal, tasteful designs: Clean lines, neutral colors, and elegant typography can give packaging a refined look without significantly raising production costs.

Eco-friendly options: Sustainable packaging not only appeals to conscious consumers but also conveys quality. Consider recyclable materials or minimalistic packaging that looks modern and thoughtful.

Avoid "economy" cues: Avoid overly bright colors or "budget" designs, which can give items an overall cheap look and feel. Instead, use subtle accents like gold or silver foil for a polished look that gives affordable products a premium touch. [20]

When customers see visually appealing packaging, they're more likely to recognize it as a quality item, albeit at a lower price point.

Limited-Edition and Seasonal Packaging

Adding limited-edition and seasonal packaging adds an element of exclusivity, making even low-cost products feel special. Limited runs or seasonal designs creates excitement, encouraging customers to buy now instead of risking missing out. Here are some ways to make it work:

Special editions for holidays or seasons: Launch holiday-themed or seasonal designs to add variety. For example, a candle brand could offer winter-themed packaging, or a skincare brand could add a *"spring collection"* of scented items.

Highlight exclusivity: Messaging like *"Limited-time only"* or *"Exclusive edition"* makes customers feel like they're getting something unique. This approach adds value by emphasizing that the opportunity is short-lived, turning an affordable product into a collectible.

Rotate designs: Even small changes in color schemes or packaging details every season can make customers feel they're experiencing something new and exclusive.

Create a Premium Experience on a Budget

Customers appreciate small, thoughtful touches that enhance their buying experience, and these don't have to be expensive. Adding a few personal elements to the packaging or presentation can make any item feel like a premium experience.

For instance, wrap items in tissue paper, add a branded sticker or include a reusable pouch. Simple additions make the unboxing experience feel special and show customers that care went into their purchase.

Consider adding a small *"freebie,"* like a mini skincare product or a bookmark with a paperback book purchase. These little extras create a feeling of abundance and give customers a pleasant surprise. They can also give customers a taste of another product or entire product line.

Following the purchase, a simple handwritten note or a printed card thanking the customer adds a more personal touch, making the experience feel authentic, which can leave a lasting impression. This also gives the customer a sense of personal connection to your brand.

Focusing on presentation and personalization makes even modestly priced items feel like an indulgence. Customers who experience this are more likely to view your brand as thoughtful and high-quality. With the right balance of aesthetic appeal, exclusivity, and personalized experience, you can make budget-friendly items feel indulgent and memorable.

In the next chapter, we'll discuss loyalty strategies that are specifically tailored for tough economic times. You'll learn how to boost revenue by encouraging repeat purchases, which helps small businesses thrive during economic downturns.

Chapter Four

How to Build Loyalty with Affordable Luxury

CUSTOMER LOYALTY IS VITAL for businesses. Loyal customers support brands they trust, providing a consistent, predictable revenue stream. In a recession, this creates a critical buffer against market volatility.

In this chapter, you'll see how to build lasting loyalty by tapping into the appeal of affordable luxuries and positioning your brand as a trusted source of comfort and joy. By understanding what keeps your customers coming back, you can build relationships that go beyond single purchases.

The Psychology Behind Repeat Purchases

Small purchases provide a sense of routine, reward, and comfort, making them more than just a product; they become a source of emotional relief. This intrinsic appeal drives repeat purchases, as customers turn to these small indulgences as regular "feel-good" moments in their lives.

Create a "Feel-Good" Experience

Affordable luxuries create a strong emotional connection with your brand by creating consistent, positive experie nces—a.k.a. *"feel-good"* moments. When customers rely on your product or service for a brief respite of enjoyment or comfort, your brand becomes embedded into their daily routine, creating deep-rooted loyalty.

This *"feel-good"* experience isn't just about the product itself—it's about the overall experience with your brand, from packaging to customer service to the brand's core message of care and connection. Each interaction reinforces your brand's role in supporting their well-being, creating emotional loyalty that feels more like an ongoing relationship than a single purchase.

Why Consumers Flock to Brands They Trust

In times of uncertainty, consumers buy from brands that feel familiar, reliable, and trustworthy. In addition to product quality, loyal customers cherish certain brands because they feel valued and understood in return. They know what to expect and appreciate a level of consistency, which serves as a comforting anchor when life otherwise feels unpredictable.

By offering products that feel rewarding and providing attentive, empathetic customer service, you build a foundation of trust and familiarity. As a result, this emotional connection becomes the backbone of customer loyalty.

The Lipstick Effect in Your Loyalty Program

Loyalty programs that reward frequent, low-cost purchases can further drive consistent revenue and deepen customer relationships. By creating a loyalty program that aligns with the lipstick effect, you can encourage repeat purchases of products that represent affordable luxuries.

Focus on Frequent, Low-Cost Purchases

Traditional loyalty programs often focus on high-value spending, but when customers are cautious with their budgets, it's essential to shift the focus to rewarding smaller, regular purchases. Crafting a loyalty program that values frequency over transaction size helps to keep your brand top-of-mind and encourages regular repeat purchases.

Design your loyalty program with achievable rewards in mind. Customers should feel rewarded for regular smaller purchases rather than needing to save up for a larger reward. This makes it easy to see progress and to stay motivated.

Similarly, you can encourage the purchase of "lipstick" products by aligning loyalty rewards with the items customers will most likely purchase during more challenging economic times.

Examples of Loyalty Perks

Loyalty programs are personal, memorable and make customers feel appreciated. Here are some ideas for structuring your loyalty program to make it more appealing:

Free product after a set number of purchases: Reward customers with a free item after a certain number of purchases—such as a complimentary coffee, candle, or small dessert.

Exclusive access to limited-edition items: In your email marketing campaigns, offer loyal customers early or exclusive access to seasonal or limited-edition products, giving them a “first look” at new product launches. This sense of exclusivity makes them feel rewarded and special, enhancing their brand experience.

Discounts on future purchases: Provide discounts that can be applied to future buys, like 10% off the next visit or a *"treat yourself"* discount for special occasions.

Loyalty programs tailored to frequent, low-cost purchases directly align with the lipstick effect, making shopping with your business a consistent part of your customers' lives.

Personalized Offers and Exclusive Benefits

Personalized offers and exclusive benefits can also make loyal customers feel uniquely valued, reinforcing their emotional bond with your products. By using customer data to tailor rewards, offering exclusive access to special products, and celebrating customer milestones, you create meaningful experiences that promote long-term loyalty.

Use Customer Data to Personalize Rewards

Using customer data to provide rewards can make loyalty programs feel highly personal, showing customers that their preferences are noticed and appreciated. Personalized offers enhance the customer experience, making each interaction with your brand more meaningful.

Tailor discounts based on purchase history: Use purchase data to create targeted discounts or exclusive offers on items that align with each customer's interests.

Recommend new products based on past preferences: Suggest items similar to products customers have previously purchased. Phrasing like, *"Since you loved our* [frequently purchased product], *try our* [new product]," shows you understand their tastes.

Send timely offers for favorite products: Remind customers about items they love with current promotions or seasonal discounts. For instance, *"Enjoy 15% off your favorite coffee blend this month"* encourages a return purchase by emphasizing your familiarity with their preferences.

By personalizing rewards, you create a loyalty experience that feels personal, attentive, and relevant, making each customer feel genuinely valued.

Exclusive Access to New or Limited-Edition Products

Similarly, providing loyal customers with early or exclusive access to new products or limited editions can make them feel like VIPs, increasing the likelihood of repeat purchases and reinforcing a sense of belonging.

Consider offering loyal customers a *"sneak peek"* of upcoming products before they're released to the public. An email saying, *"You're invited to try our* [new product] *first!"* creates a sense of excitement and appreciation, making customers feel like valued insiders.

Likewise, providing exclusive access to limited-edition products or seasonal specials, like one-time-only product launches, can drive demand while making loyal customers feel rewarded for their ongoing support.

For an even more personalized touch, consider holding invite-only virtual events where top-tier customers can interact with new products or get a behind-the-scenes look. These types of experiences make customers feel like a valued part of the brand.

Celebrate Customer Milestones

Recognizing important milestones in a customer's journey with your brand also adds a personal touch to the loyalty experience. These small gestures show customers they're remembered and appreciated, further strengthening their emotional bond with your brand.

Celebrate the anniversary of the customer's first purchase or loyalty program sign-up with a small reward. For instance, *"Thanks for being with us for a year! Enjoy a free* [complementary item] *on us"* recognizes their loyalty and encourages continued engagement.

Reward customers when they reach loyalty milestones, such as their 10th or 20th purchase, with a free gift or exclusive discount. Highlighting these achievements makes them feel proud of their participation, adding a sense of accomplishment to their loyalty journey.

Use Feedback and Personalization

To build lasting loyalty, it's essential to create a customer experience that feels personal, responsive, and genuinely attentive to changing customer needs. You can do this by actively gathering and acting on feedback and tailoring communications to reflect individual preferences.

Involve Customers in Your Brand

Inviting customers to share their thoughts and suggestions gives you valuable insights into their needs and strengthens their connection to your brand. When customers feel personally involved in shaping your brand, they're more likely to view it as collaborative and customer-centric.

Use surveys, post-purchase emails, or social media polls to invite customers to share their opinions on your products and services. Questions like, *"What items would you love to see next?"* or *"How can we improve your experience?"* show customers that their opinions matter.

When considering new products or features, ask your customers for input with exclusive previews or surveys. For example, *"Help us choose our next seasonal scent!"* makes customers invested in your brand and part of the decision-making process.

Finally, consider inviting a limited group of loyal customers to provide feedback and suggestions on new product ideas. This involvement not only deepens loyalty but also gives you early insights into how your core audience will respond to new products.

Create Personalized Marketing Campaigns

In addition to involving customers in shaping your brand, personalized marketing campaigns create a sense of familiarity and show customers that their individual preferences are recognized. Segmenting your communications based on purchase history, browsing behavior, or product interests ensures that messages feel relevant and tailored.

Use customer data to segment email campaigns and target customers with recommendations or offers that reflect their previous purchases and buying preferences. For instance, if a customer frequently buys scented candles, send them an email introducing new or seasonal candle scents.

Divide customers into interest groups (e.g., *"skincare enthusiasts"* or *"home decor lovers"*) and send tailored emails that feature products and tips relevant to each group. This strategic approach makes communications feel curated and personal—directly aligning with their unique preferences.

Use data to offer individual discounts on customers' favorite items or on products they've shown interest in. Phrases like, *"A special offer on something you love!"* or *"We noticed you've had your eye on this item"* make customers feel deeply understood.

By personalizing customer emails, you show that you're familiar with their preferences, making each interaction with your brand feel unique and special. This helps to enhance customer loyalty by creating an experience that's tailored, attentive, and genuinely customer-focused. This sends the message that you truly value and understand your customers.

Turn Loyal Customers into Brand Advocates

Loyal customers who believe in your brand are your best (and least expensive) marketers. By empowering these customers to share their experiences and rewarding them for spreading the word, you can expand your reach organically, building a larger community of engaged customers. This is a powerful way to attract new customers through authentic, trusted recommendations.

Create a Brand Ambassador Program

Formal advocacy programs, like referral or ambassador initiatives, motivate loyal customers to actively promote your brand to friends, family, and followers. When customers receive clear incentives to share their love for your brand, they're more likely to do so consistently, helping you reach new audiences through trusted referrals.

Set up your referral program in a way that rewards loyal customers for bringing in new customers. For example, offer both the referrer and the new customer a discount on their next purchase, creating a win-win that encourages both parties to support your brand.

Alternatively, consider creating an ambassador program. Ambassadors generally receive exclusive perks, such as early access to new products, in exchange for sharing their experiences with your brand on social media or participating in occasional promotional activities.

Make it easy for customers to join the program and explain clearly how it works. Offer rewards that are meaningful yet manageable, to ensure participants feel incentivized without incurring a heavy expense to your business.

A structured advocacy program provides a framework to promote your brand actively, turning customer enthusiasm into a powerful growth tool.

Encourage Word-of-Mouth Referrals

Word-of-mouth referrals are one of the oldest, most trusted forms of marketing. By offering small, thoughtful rewards for successful referrals, you can further motivate customers to share their positive experiences and make it easier for new customers to join your community.

One popular method is to reward customers with loyalty points, small discounts, or a free item after a successful referral. For each subsequent referral, give customers an accumulating reward, such as an increasing discount or a free larger item after three referrals. This builds excitement as customers see each referral, which brings them closer to a tangible reward.

Encourage customers to post about their experience on social media by offering a discount or extra loyalty points to tag your brand. This can generate additional interest from their network, and even one positive post can attract new customers who trust the recommendation.

These referral incentives reward loyalty while enabling customers to introduce your brand to new potential customers in an authentic, friendly way.

Celebrate Customer Stories and Reviews

Showcasing customer stories, reviews, and social media posts is another powerful way to turn loyal customers into advocates. By featuring their experiences, you inspire new customers to see your brand through the eyes of real, satisfied users.

Be sure to share customer testimonials on your website, social media, and email campaigns. Authentic quotes build trust and make prospective customers feel more confident trying your brand.

Additionally, encourage customers to tag your brand or use a branded hashtag when posting about their favorite products. Reposting these images and stories on social media shows that you value and appreciate your customers.

Consider dedicating a section of your emails or social media feeds to spotlight a loyal customer each month, sharing their story and favorite products. Not only does this celebrate their loyalty, but it also strengthens their personal connection to your brand. By recognizing and celebrating customer stories, you make your loyal customers feel valued and turn them into advocates who proudly share their experiences with others.

Turning loyal customers into brand advocates amplifies your reach and builds trust with new audiences. With advocacy programs, word-of-mouth incentives, and customer stories, you create a community of enthusiastic supporters who help your brand grow organically and authentically.

In the next chapter, we'll look beyond the lipstick effect to examine strategies for sustaining growth post-recession. You'll learn how to retain loyal customers as the economy shifts and prepare for new opportunities, setting the stage for continued success and resilience as consumer spending stabilizes.

Chapter Five

Pivot From Recession to Growth

As economic conditions improve, it's time to shift the focus from survival to sustainable growth. In times of recovery, the challenge often lies in moving beyond recession-era tactics and developing a strategy that drives expansion while maintaining the loyalty built in tougher times.

In this chapter, you'll see how to retain loyal customers who support your brand through downturns and keep them engaged as the economy recovers—positioning your brand for long-term growth.

How to Sustain Customer Relationships

It's crucial to maintain the strong customer relationships built during recessions, quickly adapting to customers' changing needs while maintaining their loyalty. This means transitioning from a focus on affordable luxuries to a broader range of products, which requires careful planning and attention to customer preferences.

Stay Connected to Loyal Customers

Keeping your customers engaged as their spending patterns shift is vital to retaining their loyalty. Regular, thoughtful communication and exclusive offers can reinforce the emotional connection they feel with your brand.

Consistently communicate through email newsletters, social media, or loyalty program updates. Share relevant content, such as product tips or behind-the-scenes stories, to keep customers connected.

Reward loyal customers with exclusive deals or early access to new products. This strategy not only shows appreciation but also encourages continued engagement, reminding them of the unique value your brand offers.

By keeping the lines of communication open with your most loyal customers, you make it easier to retain their loyalty as economic conditions shift.

Acknowledge Customers' Changing Needs

Remember that as economic conditions improve, customers often develop new priorities and preferences. Adapting your product lines to reflect these shifts shows your brand's commitment to customer satisfaction.

Watch for shifts in customer preferences by paying attention to customer feedback, social media conversations, and industry trends. This will help you to stay aware of changing needs and preferences.

As budgets stabilize, some customers may be ready for larger purchases, while others may still appreciate affordable options. Providing a range of choices, such as payment plans for premium items or bundling options, ensures your products serve a range of budgets.

By adapting to customers' changing needs, you promote a feeling of support and loyalty, showing that your brand remains committed to their satisfaction and well-being. This creates a strong foundation for continued growth.

Use Data to Guide Your Long-Term Strategy

The data you gather during recessions will give you a unique perspective on customer preferences and purchasing behaviors while under financial stress. Leveraging these insights can help you create marketing strategies that also resonate with customers in a stable economy.

Start by examining which affordable products consistently performed well. They may reflect lasting customer preferences that you can incorporate into future products.

Next, look at peak shopping times and days of the week when customers were most active. This data can also help optimize marketing efforts, aligning promotional campaigns with times of high engagement.

Finally, track and analyze data on items that were purchased repeatedly to understand which products became part of customers' routines. Use this information to design loyalty programs or bundled products that support buying trends.

Using these data points, you can tailor your products and marketing strategies to align with customer habits, creating a smoother transition from recession-focused to growth-oriented planning.

Identify Core Products That Drive Loyalty

The recession may have highlighted products that consistently drove customer engagement and repeat purchases.

These "core" products can be a reliable foundation for your post-recession product lineup, reinforcing brand loyalty and meeting customer expectations.

First, identify the products that were most popular during the downturn. Consider making these items staples in your lineup, as they have proven appeal and may continue to drive sales in better economic times.

Products that were repeatedly purchased or received positive feedback are often loyalty drivers. Building your core lineup around these items can help retain loyal customers, who know they can rely on these familiar favorites.

If certain low-cost products were especially popular, consider creating variations or complementary products that expand on this success. This allows you to build on established customer preferences while offering variety.

By centering your product lineup around these loyalty-driving items, you provide customers with a familiar foundation, making it easier for them to continue engaging with your brand post-recession.

Refine Customer Experiences Based on Feedback

The feedback gathered from customers during the recession is another valuable resource for boosting loyalty. Using these insights to make long-term improvements ensures that your brand continues to deliver quality, service, and value as economic conditions shift.

Always use feedback to continually refine customer experiences, whether it's response times, communication style, or after-sales service. Empathetic and timely service should be a permanent part of your brand's experience.

Recession-era feedback may reveal customer preferences for specific product types, materials, or styles. Use these data points to prioritize improvements or expand options to better meet customer needs.

Finally, align your brand message with the values that mattered most to customers during the downturn, such as reliability, value, and care. This consistency reinforces customer trust, making them more likely to stay loyal post-recession.

By analyzing recession-era data, focusing on core products, and enhancing the customer experience, you can create a resilient, customer-focused strategy that transcends the lipstick effect. These insights help maintain a loyal customer base and strengthen your brand's ability to weather any economic climate.

Align Product Lines to Customer Preferences

As the economy changes, so do customer preferences. Expanding your product line to meet their needs drives growth and solidifies brand loyalty. This helps you grow revenue while catering to a broader range of customer needs and spending habits.

Introduce Mid-Tier Products

As customers become more comfortable with spending, mid-tier products can bridge the gap between affordable luxuries and higher-end items, providing customers with appealing options that offer both quality and value.

Start with your best-selling, lower-priced items and consider introducing mid-tier versions with enhanced features, materials, or sizes. When introducing mid-tier products, emphasize the added value and quality they offer. For instance, position these products as *"worth the investment"* due to their lasting benefits or higher-quality components.

To avoid over-investing in new products, gradually introduce mid-tier products in limited quantities or seasonal items to gauge initial customer response. This approach minimizes risk while allowing you to refine the product line based on feedback.

A mid-tier product strategy helps you cater to customers who are ready to invest a bit more in quality, giving them options that align with their spending power.

Create Premium Versions of Popular Products

For loyal customers who are ready to elevate their purchases, premium versions of recession favorites can provide an enticing upgrade. These high-end items allow customers to enjoy the products they love, now with enhanced features or with a more luxurious twist.

Invest in high-quality materials, unique packaging, or special ingredients to create premium versions of popular products. For instance, if a candle was a bestseller, introduce a premium version with a longer burn time or a custom glass container.

Market these premium items as exclusive or limited-edition offerings to create a sense of added luxury and exclusivity. This strategy appeals to customers seeking something unique that goes along with their existing favorite products.

Encourage loyal customers to try premium versions by offering early access or loyalty discounts. Customers already invested in your brand are more likely to upgrade if they feel they're getting a special version of something they already enjoy. Premium versions of product favorites allow customers to upgrade their experience, appealing to their loyalty and readiness for higher-quality items.

Expanding your product line lets you capture emerging customer preferences while maintaining flexibility. This strategy positions your brand for sustainable growth, reinforcing loyalty and establishing a product lineup that retains customers.

Adjust Marketing for Growth

As the economy starts to recover, it's time to transition your overall marketing strategy from recession-focused messaging to a growth-oriented approach. By adjusting your messaging to highlight new and upgraded items and reinforcing your brand's commitment to quality, you can appeal to both loyal customers and new ones eager to invest in reliable products.

Change Messaging for Economic Recovery

As consumer confidence begins to rebound, optimistic marketing messages create a sense of excitement and renewed energy that signals to customers that they should resume normal spending levels. Focus on positive themes that celebrate resilience and growth, while still acknowledging the value that your brand offers.

Use language that reflects a forward-looking attitude, such as *"embrace what's next"* or *"welcome new possibilities."* These phrases tap into customers' desire to move forward, helping them see your brand as part of their revived daily routines.

Show appreciation for customers who supported your brand during tough times. Messages like *"Thank you for being with us"* or *"Let's continue this journey together"* help deepen connections and retain customer loyalty as spending increases.

Even as customers start to increase their spending, affordability and value remain essential. Highlight the fact that your products deliver lasting quality and satisfaction, making them worthwhile buys for customers who still want to spend wisely.

Marketing messages that focus on themes of optimism while maintaining a focus on value help keep your brand top-of-mind for customers who are ready to increase spending but still prioritize smart, meaningful purchases.

Highlight New and Upgraded Products

As you introduce mid- to high-value products, your marketing should showcase these items as exciting additions to your lineup, appealing to both loyal customers ready to upgrade and new customers attracted by your brand's fresh, new product lineup.

Emphasize the unique features or benefits of each new product, such as premium materials, enhanced performance, or exclusive designs. Focus on how these products directly elevate the overall customer experience.

For loyal customers, introduce new products as a way to upgrade their favorite items. For new customers, highlight how these products add to your brand's core message, showing its growth and innovation.

Feature testimonials from customers who've tried and loved the new items, especially if they comment on the added quality or value. Social proof helps new products feel like trusted choices, encouraging others to explore them.

Spotlighting new and upgraded products with targeted messaging generates excitement and shows that your brand is evolving to meet the needs of its growing customer base.

Emphasize Quality, Service, and Long-Term Value

With an expanded product lineup, emphasize the quality, durability, and service that make your products a valuable investment. This helps reassure customers that they're making sound, lasting purchases as they transition back to regular spending.

Use language that reinforces the lasting value of your products, like *"crafted for quality"* or *"designed to endure."* This language helps to position your products as investments, encouraging customers to choose quality over quantity as they start to spend more freely.

Showcase your commitment to customer support, mainly any services that enhance the purchase experience, such as easy returns, dedicated customer assistance, or personalized product care guidance. Excellent service reinforces customer confidence and strengthens brand loyalty.

Position your product line as timeless rather than trendy, focusing on versatility and durability. Emphasize that your items hold their value over time, aligning with customers' desire for sustainable and reliable choices. By centering your marketing strategy on quality, service, and long-term value, you reinforce your brand's commitment to excellence, making it a trusted choice as customers' spending power grows.

With marketing messages that reflect optimism, highlight new products, and emphasize quality and value, your brand can seamlessly transition from survival mode to growth mode. This helps capture renewed interest and loyalty, setting the stage for a successful recovery and long-term success.

Continue Building Loyalty as Spending Shifts

As customers' spending habits evolve with economic recovery, maintaining and growing loyalty becomes a nuanced task. By tweaking loyalty programs, providing personalized offers, and rewarding long-term connections, you can keep existing customers while building new customer relationships.

Update Loyalty Programs to Match Buying Patterns

With customers ready to invest in higher-value purchases, loyalty programs should reflect their new spending habits. Modifying rewards and points structures can incentivize continued participation, offering rewards that recognize larger purchases.

To start, assign bigger rewards for mid- and high-tier purchases, giving customers extra incentives to purchase higher-value items. For instance, customers might earn double points for premium product purchases or for reaching a certain spending threshold.

Add loyalty tiers, such as Silver, Gold, and Platinum, with exclusive rewards at each level. These tiers encourage customers to make larger or more frequent purchases to unlock benefits such as exclusive discounts, early access to new products, or VIP treatment.

Adjust your loyalty program so that regular purchases of higher-value items are acknowledged with unique perks, like free shipping on orders over a set amount or quarterly rewards for consistent high spenders. By adjusting your loyalty program to reward increased spending, you keep it attractive to customers as their buying power increases.

Personalized Offers for Recession-Era Loyalists

Recognizing and rewarding customers who have been loyal through economic challenges is a great way to show appreciation and build deeper connections. Providing tailored incentives or exclusive offers to these customers, is a special way to recognize them and continue encouraging loyalty.

Send personalized "thank you" messages with a special discount or gift for customers who supported your brand during the downturn. A message like, *"Thanks for being with us through thick and thin—enjoy 20% off your next purchase"* adds a warm, personal touch.

Give recession-era supporters early access to new product launches, limited editions, or premium versions of popular items. This makes them feel like valued insiders, reinforcing their connection to the brand.

Based on each loyal customer's past purchase history, offer exclusive discounts on similar or complementary products. This approach not only encourages repeat purchases but also shows that you've paid attention to their preferences. Personalized offers help deepen emotional relationships with loyal customers, showing gratitude for their support during tough times and making them feel valued as spending increases.

Through adaptive loyalty programs, personalized offers for loyal customers, and milestone celebrations, you can maintain and grow customer loyalty even as spending patterns shift. These strategies ensure that your brand remains meaningful and connected to customers, creating a foundation that supports sustainable growth and customer satisfaction.

Final Thoughts

Throughout this book, we've discussed the *"lipstick effect,"* its impact on your business, and on the economy at large. The *"lipstick effect,"* while somewhat of an obscure concept to most small business owners, is a powerful phenomenon that can be leveraged for long-term growth in any economy.

Remember that recessions come and go, and more growth happens during times of economic pullback than when the economy is booming. Harnessing the *"lipstick effect"* is just one piece of a much larger puzzle.

Building a business that endures requires adaptability, a customer-centered approach, and a commitment to growth that remains steady through economic ups and downs. By focusing on customer needs, innovating thoughtfully, and preparing to adjust as conditions change, you can position your brand to thrive in both challenging and prosperous times.

Stay responsive, prioritize quality, and keep your brand vision clear, and your business will be well-equipped to navigate the future with resilience and success.

P.S. — if this book has helped you overcome a challenge or has given you some practical tips or other value, please consider leaving a review on whatever platform you purchased it on. My goal is to help as many small business owners as possible.

Once again, thank you for allowing me to be a part of your journey.

With Love and Gratitude,

Donovan Garett

DONOVAN GARETT MEDIA CO.

1. "Lipstick Effect Definition," Investopedia, https://www.investopedia.com/terms/l/lipstick-effect.asp
2. "The Compensatory Consumer Behavior Model: How self-discrepancies drive consumer behavior," Journal of Consumer Psychology, Volume 27, Issue 1
3. "Why do we think less about some purchases than others?" The Decision Lab, https://www.beactionlab.org/articles/
4. "'Little luxuries': The affordable treats driving consumer spending," BBC, https://www.bbc.com/worklife/article/20240104-little-luxuries-the-affordable-treats-driving-consumer-spending
5. "With Recession Threatening, The Lipstick Effect Kicks In And Lipstick Sales Rise," Forbes, https://www.forbes.com/sites/pamdanziger/2022/06/01/with-inflation-rising-the-lipstick-effect-kicks-in-and-lipstick-sales-rise/?sh=1d3bfd301276
6. "Do Economic Downturns Make Us Buy More Makeup?" Texas Christian University College of Science and Engineering, https://cse.tcu.edu/stories/posts/lipstick-effect.php
7. *"For Beauty on Duty" - The Power of Lipstick in WW2,* The Seamstress of Bloomsbury, https://theseamstressofbloomsbury.co.uk/blogs/seamstress-blog/for-beauty-on-duty-the-power-of-lipstick-in-ww2
8. "What is the Lipstick Effect?" Glenmont Consulting, https://glenmont.co/what-is-the-lipstick-effect
9. "The lipstick effect during COVID-19 lockdown," National Library of Medicine, https://pmc.ncbi.nlm.nih.gov/articles/PMC9636953
10. "Why Celebrating Small Wins Matters," Harvard University, https://summer.harvard.edu/blog/why-celebrating-small-wins-matters/

11. "Little Luxuries Can Make a Big Difference for Your Mental Health," Verywell Mind, https://www.verywellmind.com/the-big-mental-health-benefits-of-little-luxuries-8637790

12. "For consumers, splurges aren't just lipstick," Deloitte, https://www2.deloitte.com/us/en/insights/industry/retail-distribution/consumer-behavior-trends-state-of-the-consumer-tracker/splurge-spending-inflation-lipstick-index.html

13. "Affordable Indulgences and Male Consumer Behavior," Harvard Business Review, https://hbr.org

14. "Americans are comfort eating potato chips, popcorn, and pretzels as economic anxiety rises and recession looms," Business Insider, https://www.businessinsider.com/americans-comfort-eat-snacks-frito-lay-cheetos-doritos-recession-2023-2

15. "The Lipstick Effect: Why Consumers Spend on Small Luxuries in Tough Times," LinkedIn, https://www.linkedin.com/pulse/lipstick-effect-why-consumers-spend-small-luxuries-tough-gunton-zqssc/

16. "Gen Z and the "Dupe" Phenomena," Fedup Foods, https://www.fedupfoods.co/insights/gen-z-and-the-dupe-phenomena

17. "Experience Over Goods: The Millennial Shift in Spending," Business.com, https://www.business.com/articles/experience-over-goods-the-millennial-shift-in-spending/

18. "Conscious Consumerism: What Is It? Where Did It Come From?" BuiltIn, https://builtin.com/articles/conscious-consumerism

19. "The Psychology of Pricing: Understanding Consumer Perception," Journal of Consumer Research, https://www.jcr.org

20. "Affordable Luxury Packaging: How to Achieve a High-End Look," Packaging Digest, https://www.packagingdigest.com

Made in the USA
Monee, IL
05 November 2026

67962921R00052